IMAGES
of America

WESTERN
KANKAKEE COUNTY

These Norton Township farmers joined together for a barn-raising in 1916. Farming has been the foundation of Kankakee County since the first settlers arrived in the 1830s. (Author's collection.)

ON THE COVER: Labor Day celebrations in Herscher always started with a ceremony at the World War I monument, which was in the intersection of Main Street and Kankakee Avenue. This picture is from the late 1940s. The state made the village take down the monument in 1963 because it was a traffic safety hazard. A new memorial was built in Village Park. (Author's collection.)

IMAGES
of America

WESTERN KANKAKEE COUNTY

Jim Ridings

Copyright © 2021 by Jim Ridings
ISBN 978-1-5402-4894-7

Published by Arcadia Publishing
Charleston, South Carolina

Library of Congress Control Number: 2021935785

For all general information, please contact Arcadia Publishing:
Telephone 843-853-2070
Fax 843-853-0044
E-mail sales@arcadiapublishing.com
For customer service and orders:
Toll-Free 1-888-313-2665

Visit us on the Internet at www.arcadiapublishing.com

Contents

Acknowledgments		6
About the Author		6
Introduction		7
1.	Bonfield and Salina Township	11
2.	Buckingham	25
3.	Cabery	33
4.	Clarke City and Coal Mining	53
5.	Essex	55
6.	Goodrich and Pilot Township	63
7.	Herscher	71
8.	Irwin and Otto Township	105
9.	Lehigh	113
10.	Limestone	117
11.	Reddick	131
12.	Union Hill and Norton Township	149

Acknowledgments

There have been many people who have contributed to the history of our area; too many to list them all here. Unless otherwise indicated, the pictures in this book are from the author's collection, which also is in the archives of the museum at the Herscher Area Historical Society.

About the Author

Jim Ridings was born in Joliet, Illinois. He earned a degree in journalism from Southern Illinois University at Carbondale with a minor in history. He was a reporter for the *Daily Times* in Ottawa and the *Beacon-News* in Aurora and won more than a dozen awards for investigative reporting at both newspapers, from the Associated Press, United Press International, Copley Press, Illinois Press Association, and other organizations. Ridings was presented a Studs Terkel Humanities Service bronze medal from the Illinois Humanities Council in 2006. He is the author of 30 books of Illinois history, including *Small Justice, Len Small: Governors and Gangsters, Cardiff, County West,* and *Wild Kankakee*. Several of his books have won awards from the Illinois State Historical Society.

Introduction

The foundation of Kankakee County has always been farming. However, it was the coming of the railroads that established the county and most of its towns.

Along the path of a railroad line, settlements, churches, and schools were started. A town usually became established with the building of a station (depot). People wanted to live near a railroad station. It meant an easy ride to other towns instead of a long and hard ride by buggy or wagon. It meant access to other places across the nation wherever trains went. It meant daily mail and freight shipments. It meant prosperity.

Railroads even made the decisions that formed Kankakee County and set Kankakee as the county seat.

This area was a part of Will and Iroquois Counties. An election was held in April 1853 to form a new county. Officials in Iroquois County claimed there was fraud at the polls—that too many votes had been cast in the Limestone area because Illinois Central Railroad laborers had been brought in to vote illegally. An Iroquois County judge threw out the Limestone votes; an appeal was filed, and the Limestone votes were declared valid. Questions about fraudulent voting in Limestone came up again two months later to decide the location of the county seat. The Illinois Central wanted the county seat at its settlement of Kankakee Depot, which was nothing more than the start of grading for railroad tracks. Quarrymen, railroad workers, and other nonresidents voted in Limestone, probably more than once, and their ballots were enough to make Kankakee Depot the county seat. The first board of supervisors meeting on July 18, 1853, was in Momence, because there were no buildings in Kankakee.

Kankakee County was divided into six townships: Yellowhead, Momence, Bourbonnais, Rockville, Aroma, and Limestone. Limestone Township once included all of what now is Salina and Pilot Townships and part of Otto Township. In 1855, Norton and Essex Townships were changed from Vermilion County to Kankakee County.

Every town in western Kankakee County became established only because a railroad decided to build a station. In 1878, the Illinois Central line went west from Kankakee to Bloomington. Irwin, Herscher, Buckingham, and Cabery all owe their existence to the Illinois Central building a station at their settlement. The Wabash Railroad and the Indiana-Illinois-Iowa Railroad (the "Three-I") solidified Union Hill and Reddick.

Other settlements died when the railroad bypassed them. Eldridgeville was a settlement that hoped to become a village; however, the Illinois Central decided to route its path a little to the west instead of going through Eldridgeville. The decision meant Cabery became a town and Eldridgeville disappeared. The Kankakee & Seneca Railroad made Frieling into a town and then made it vanish when rail service ended in 1933. The same railroad made the village of Verkler change its name to Bonfield.

In 1882, the Illinois Central extended a spur line from Buckingham to Clarke City and Tracy, which allowed coal mining to prosper.

Many settlements were known by the name of the railroad station, such as Irwin Station.

In the 1920s and 1930s, the popularity of the automobile brought the paving of roads between towns all across America. That resulted in a decline in passenger train service and freight service and a dramatic decline of small towns.

Places like Herscher, Reddick, Cabery, and others had a variety of businesses, all of which provided needed essentials. A wagon ride from Cabery to Kankakee and back would take all day and was hard work. Automobiles and roads provided freedom and the ability to go to bigger cities.

That is probably what will surprise young readers the most—how many businesses and services were available in their towns more than 100 years ago, compared to the few that remain today.

The fertile soil and the flat land made farming the ideal choice for settlers. Life on the farm in the early 20th century was different from today. Before harvesting machines in the 1930s, husking corn was done by hand. A long day's work might bring 100 bushels. One old farmer told me in the 1990s that as a child in the 1920s and 1930s, he would drive horses to power the grain elevator, and he also drove loose pigs and cattle down the road to the stockyards in Buckingham to be put on the train to be taken to market in Chicago. In the early 1900s, corn rows were planted 40 inches apart to allow for horse teams. Today, they are planted four inches apart.

In the Depression years of the 1930s, many farmers earned very little. However, the farmer raised or made most of what he needed, and the cost of other things was low. Of course, farm profits also were low. In 1931, eggs sold for 6¢ a dozen, corn was 15¢ a bushel, and hogs sold for $2.50 per hundredweight.

Life on the farm meant getting up at dawn and doing a few hours of chores before walking a mile to school. There were more chores after school. At home, there was no internet, no computer, no video games, no movies, and no television. The family was lucky to have a telephone or a radio in the 1930s. When TV entered homes in the 1950s, there were only four channels, all in black and white.

The home likely had no electricity or plumbing. That meant illumination by lamplight (or perhaps electricity from a Delco battery system). Heating the house was done by stoking the stove with coal or corncobs. And the bathroom was a trip to the outhouse behind the house on a cold night. A Sears catalogue or corncobs served as toilet paper.

If you lived on a farm, you likely did the plowing with horsepower—the kind that had a tail, not an engine. If you wanted chicken or ham for dinner, you had to go to the barnyard and butcher the animal yourself.

Children would be excused from school at certain times of the year to help with farm work. Neighbors could always be counted upon for harvesting crops or other work when a farmer died or was ill.

Rural schools were one-room schoolhouses where all eight grades were taught together by one teacher. When one grade was being taught its lessons, the other children studied. An advantage of this system was that the pupils heard lessons from the other grades, allowing them to review material from previous years or get a head start on the following year's lessons. The west end of the room was partitioned for a cob and coal area; the east end had cloak rooms. A pump outside the door provided water. In the back of the room was a table for the water bucket and dipper. Lunch was brought in a pail or bucket. There was no electricity and no indoor plumbing. The bathroom was an outhouse in the back of the schoolhouse.

Rural schools were located within every two sections so children could walk to school, usually less than two miles. The schools were in session eight months of the year. The teacher, in addition to holding classes for all eight grades in all subjects, hauled coal and lit the stove in the morning, conducted art and music classes, put on holiday programs, and gave first aid. A teacher was given no personal or sick days; she was there every day or her meager pay was docked to pay a substitute.

In 1949, both Herscher and Reddick planned to form unit districts. Herscher got to the courthouse first and was first on the ballot. The referendum was approved, bringing in all of Pilot and Salina Townships, the Buckingham School District, parts of Limestone and Essex Townships, and parts of Ford and Iroquois Counties.

There were several destructive tornadoes in western Kankakee County. A twister on July 17, 1903, blew down the barn on the Pat Breen farm west of Cabery, burying three Breen sons in hay and killing 17-year-old Frank. It also struck a mile south of Irwin, demolishing many houses and barns. Fields and orchards were flattened, many farm animals were killed, and 30 windmills were destroyed.

Then there was the tornado of November 11, 1911. It was unseasonably warm when suddenly, just after 6:00 p.m., a tornado carved a path from the southwest. A number of farm buildings, school buildings, and stores were damaged or destroyed. The tornado leveled the buildings on the Peter Kersch farm north of Cabery. Sixteen-year-old Frank Kersch was killed when a flying timber hit him in the head. His mother and older brother were injured. After the storm went through, the temperature dropped 60 degrees as the rain poured for three hours before turning to snow.

A stronger tornado on April 21, 1912, hit Reddick, Union Hill, Bonfield, and Limestone. The tornado blew down farmhouses, schools, windmills, and barns and killed livestock in great numbers along its path. The tornado obliterated a farmhouse one mile west of Reddick, killing Nelson Hulse, his wife, Phebe, and their two daughters, Irene and Bessie. Finnette Anna Hawkins and her daughter Nettie Jay were killed when a barn blew down on them in Limestone Township.

A tornado on April 2, 1982, damaged several houses and farm buildings in Irwin, Essex, and Reddick. St. James Catholic Church in Irwin was destroyed.

There are a number of towns in western Kankakee County (and all across America) that no longer exist. Clarke City, Tracy, and Oklahoma were coal-mining towns in Essex Township that began in the 1880s and lasted only as long as the mines operated.

Gronso was a stop on the Wabash Railroad line two miles north of Reddick named for the man who gave the railroad the right of way through his land. Trains stopped there to pick up milk and passengers. Dickey's Siding was in Pilot Township, where Sylvester Dickey built a grain elevator and a store.

Eldridgeville was on the county line just east of Cabery. It died when the Illinois Central bypassed it when it went from Kankakee to Bloomington in 1878. Frieling was named for the owner of the land in Salina Township.

Grand Prairie was northwest of Buckingham. It had a post office from 1855 to 1860, a blacksmith shop, and some farm buildings. The place later was known as Norton Village.

Hawkins was a railroad depot and post office in Limestone Township along the Kankakee & Seneca (K&S) Railroad line. Greenwich Station was just north of Route 17 in Limestone Township. The K&S Railroad ran through there, and there was a grain elevator and a phosphate bin.

Carrow was in Pilot Township just east of Goodrich. When the Three-I Railroad was built in 1882, a station was set up along the line. This first was called Cagwin and later Carrow.

Pogsonville was two miles north of Buckingham. When the railroad line went through Buckingham in 1878, the church and other buildings were moved to Buckingham.

This was a wedding party or other social event at the Norwegian Lutheran Church in the 1890s, when the church was located southwest of Herscher in Pilot Township. From left to right are (first row) Milda Olsen; (second row) Ella Thorson and Ida Peterson; (third row) Emma Peterson, Anna Olsen, and Gertrude Olsen; (fourth row) Carrie Thorson and Della Thorson; (fifth row) Hattie Isaacson.

One

Bonfield and Salina Township

The village of Bonfield originally was named Verkler.

John Verkler was born in 1849. He and his brother Sam platted the town of Verkler in 1882.

The people of Verkler knew that the path of a railroad line and the building of a station could make a town, and they were anxious when the Kankakee & Seneca Railroad announced plans in 1881 to go through Salina Township. There was competition for where a depot would be built, with three possible sites. The first was the Henry and the Harker land on the east border of the township. The second was Verkler. The third was the Henry Wingert farm, a mile west of Verkler.

Thomas Bonfield, an attorney for the railroad, was in charge of locating stations and obtaining the right of way. In an account written by local historian Burt Burroughs (1862–1934), the decision was made by Bonfield based on cold, hard cash. Burroughs wrote that Bonfield made his proposition: "Before anyone got a station, there would have to be laid down in cold cash the sum of $2,000." The Verkler brothers and others went to neighboring farmers and secured pledges toward that amount.

They took the pledges to Bonfield, who "made it clear that a subscription list was not negotiable paper." He insisted that the people of Verkler pay him $2,000 in cash now, and they could later collect the pledges themselves.

The money was paid, and Verkler got the railroad station. John Verkler surveyed part of his farm into town lots and started selling them.

The town was recorded at the Kankakee County Courthouse in January 1882 as the village of Verkler. However, after the station was built, a freight train pulled up to the station platform with a large wooden sign that spelled "Bonfield."

That was the name on the depot that people saw when they got on and off the train. When the village was incorporated in 1888, the name became Bonfield.

The price for getting a rail station and keeping the village alive was a cash bribe and a name change.

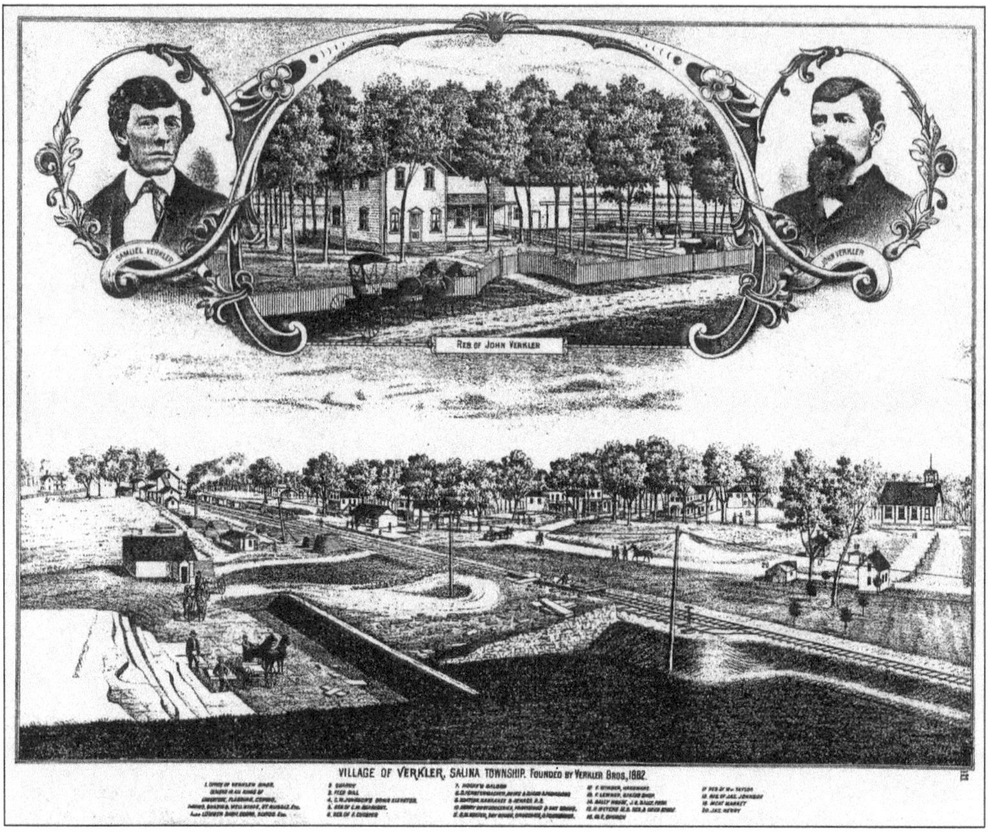

The village of Verkler is pictured in 1882.

Pictured is Smith Street, looking east, with Fred Mau and his mail wagon. Mau delivered mail for 37 years, from 1920 to 1957.

Salina Township thresher men are seen here in 1933. The township was named for the salty composition of the land. Much of the land northwest toward the Kankakee River had to be drained in order to be cultivated. The township was organized on April 27, 1854, after being carved from Limestone Township.

The war memorial in Bonfield was dedicated on September 23, 1921.

These are Dunn School students in rural Salina Township in 1946. Seven small rural schools consolidated in 1947. They were Geelan, Vining, McGillivary, Dunn, Sauerman, Bossert, and Bonfield. All the pupils attended Bonfield Grade School, since the building was large enough for all of them.

Children had fun at baseball games, such as this one at a church picnic in the 1920s.

The Bonfield Cornet Band is pictured around 1900.

The henhouse at Cal Snyder's farm was made of cornhusks. Cal is on one knee to the side. The farm was where the grade school is now.

The village built this stone school building in 1885 and added a primary room in 1889. The building burned down in January 1920. The Methodist parsonage was used for classrooms until a new school was built in the fall of 1921.

The Bonfield Grade School class of 1915 is seen here.

The Bonfield Evangelical Church Sunday school class posed for this portrait in 1923.

Bonfield Grade School students are seen in 1930.

The 1911 tornado caused a lot of damage, including to Dan Rice's farm near Bonfield.

This was Mike Kline's blacksmith shop in Bonfield. In 1929, Bonfield proved that every vote counts. In the election for mayor, A.C. Shreffler edged John Buente by two votes, 79 to 77. Buente disputed the result. A judge threw out two votes and declared the election a tie. Shreffler and Buente drew lots in court to decide the election. Buente won.

Pictured here is Bonfield High School in 1922. A two-year high school course started in 1921, which was extended to three years in 1932. A gymnasium was built in 1934. The high school was discontinued in 1941, and students went to neighboring high schools. Reddick High School was the choice of most students. In 1949, Bonfield and Salina Township became part of Herscher Community Unit School District 2. This was an unpopular idea in Salina Township, where the vote was 201-95 against joining Herscher's district. However, the vote in the entire proposed district was approved, so Salina Township was included. Bonfield had a chance to establish its own community high school district at an election on March 16, 1940; it would have consolidated nearby areas outside established districts including Salina, Limestone, Pilot, Essex, and Rockville Townships. But the measure failed by three votes, 342 to 339.

Bonfield, a town of approximately 400 people, has three Methodist churches. Bonfield Evangelical United Methodist Church traces its beginnings to 1847, when services were held in Peter Shreffler's home. A church was built in 1867. The present church (pictured) was built on Smith Street in 1918.

First United Methodist Church dates to 1860. People met in homes and schools until a church was built in 1881 on Church Street on land donated by John Verkler.

Grand Prairie United Methodist Church started as part of a five-church circuit in 1858. A church was built in 1868; a larger church (pictured) was built in 1910.

Zion Lutheran Church–Bonfield began when German Lutheran settlers in the 1850s held services in private homes. A church was built in 1861. A second (and present) church was built in 1881.

Evangelical Association camp meetings began in 1854. Beginning in 1855, the camp meetings were on John Hertz's property, known as Hertz Grove, a mile southwest of Bonfield. They were held there for the next 135 years. Hundreds of people would come from many miles. The last of the Hertz Grove tent meetings was in July 1988.

When the Kankakee & Seneca Railroad line went through Salina Township in 1882, a depot was built on the Frieling family property. Located between Bonfield and Essex, Frieling had stores, a popular dance hall, and more. There was nothing left by the time the railroad ceased operations in 1933.

Chester and Son Hardware also had an undertaking (funeral) business, a common combination with a furniture maker.

In 1879, the Verklers opened a quarry, which later was a popular swimming spot. The village cancelled the Salina Sportsmen's Club's lease on the property in 2004 when the club would not buy the amount of insurance the village required. The matter went to court in 2005, and the village won. It ended the Salina Sportsman's Club, and the quarry was closed to swimmers.

East Avenue in Bonfield is pictured here in the early 1900s.

West Avenue in Bonfield is seen here a century ago.

Two

BUCKINGHAM

The village of Buckingham was named for Ebenezer Buckingham, a Chicago investor who helped bring the Illinois Central Railroad through in 1878. However, a settlement goes back to 1854, when Alex Campbell bought land from the government. The land changed hands several times until James and G.W. Townsend deeded 15 acres for a right of way for the railroad in 1878.

William Conrow started a cheese factory in 1877 and a newspaper in 1879. He also helped obtain the right of way for the railroad. Within a short time, a depot, stores, a stockyard, and a warehouse were built. The railroad conveyed all the land it did not need to Ebenezer Buckingham.

The plat of the town was certified on October 14, 1878, by county surveyor James Croswell, but the village was not incorporated until July 1902.

A fire in 1885 destroyed nearly all of the businesses in Buckingham. The loss was estimated at $100,000.

The small settlement of Pogsonville, two miles north of Buckingham, ended after the railroad and depot were built in Buckingham. A Methodist church and houses from Pogsonville were moved to Buckingham.

At one time, there were two post offices in the Buckingham area. Grand Prairie Post Office at Norton Village, northwest of the present site of Buckingham, was established in 1855. Buckingham had a post office by the late 1870s.

Col. Levi G. Nutt (1865–1938) is the most famous person to come from Buckingham. He became the agent in charge of all divisions of the US Internal Revenue Department. Nutt later organized and became the first chief of the Narcotics Information Bureau.

William Van Doren (1823–1903) was a Norton Township farmer and Methodist minister. His son Charles practiced medicine in Buckingham and Herscher. Charles had two sons: Mark, who won a Pulitzer Prize in 1939 for poetry, and Carl, who was an author; both were professors at Columbia University. Mark's son Charles became famous in 1957 when he was at the center of the TV quiz show scandals as a contestant who was given answers in advance.

The Illinois Central Railroad station in Buckingham is seen in its early days.

William G. Smith built a magnificent house in Buckingham. Smith was a farmer, and was Norton Township supervisor from 1889 to 1892.

This view of the farm of Alvin and Laura Gaus, south of Buckingham, is seen from the top of a barn in 1950.

The Haight and Mahood general store is on the right. Next is a hardware store, a furniture and undertaking place, a bank, a barbershop, a restaurant and post office, and the Methodist church steeple in the distance.

Buckingham Methodist Church was organized in 1865. A school, built in 1867 at Pogsonville, was moved to Buckingham in 1881. There was dissention in 1898 regarding where the new church should be built, so part of the congregation left and formed the Buckingham Presbyterian Church. The new building (pictured) was dedicated on May 28, 1899.

The first church burned down on January 18, 1948. A new church (pictured) was built and was dedicated on Sunday, May 15, 1949. Membership at the church declined, and it closed in 1997.

Lil Bibler's Hotel was one of several hotels in Buckingham when it was a thriving town.

The Buckingham Public School was built in 1884. It was torn down in 1930 and replaced with a brick building.

This was Elm Street in Buckingham in 1909. The church steeple on the right belonged to the Buckingham Presbyterian Church.

The Modern Woodmen Hall in Buckingham is seen here. Farmers State Bank of Buckingham was robbed on September 10, 1918, and again on February 3, 1921. Both times, the robbers used nitroglycerin to blow open the vault. A third robbery occurred on October 4, 1929, when a gunman got away with $1,052. The bank closed for good in the Great Depression of the early 1930s.

The Buckingham Broom Brigade consisted of women who supported the campaign of Benjamin Harrison for president in 1888. They attended a rally of 15,000 people in Kankakee.

Reed Brothers Hardware in Buckingham was a thriving business.

Here is a view taken from the top of a grain elevator. The Methodist Episcopal church is in the distance at left.

Three

CABERY

Cabery originally was known informally as Four Corners. In its early days, it was little more than a general store at the intersection of two wagon trails on the prairie.

According to a Pilot Township church history from 1920, this area was known to Catholics in the 1860s as Paradis, named for the family from Luxembourg who settled in the area.

Cabery is in two counties. Main Street is the dividing line. North of Main Street is Norton Township in Kankakee County; south of Main Street is Rogers Township in Ford County. An early newspaper account noted, "Tis many a Ford County deputy, armed with a subpoena, traveled the long fifty-odd miles back home with the document unserved when the subject merely walked across the street to comparative safety."

Cabery's existence was guaranteed when the Illinois Central Railroad went through in 1878 and built a station.

The local Masonic lodge gave the town its name. Walter Colton was in charge of purchasing furniture for the lodge. John R. Caberry of Chicago was a furniture salesman. Caberry was a Mason, and he donated $200 worth of furniture to the local lodge in 1869. The lodge was so grateful that it petitioned the grand lodge to have the lodge named for Caberry. They were informed that a lodge could not be named for a living person, so the name became Norton Masonic Lodge.

However, the local postmaster named his office Caberry. When the town was incorporated in 1881, the postmaster insisted that the name of the town be Caberry. Some years later, one "r" in the name was dropped.

John Caberry was a wealthy man when he made his donation. Many years later, he suffered a financial setback. The lodge was prosperous enough at that time to send him $200 when he needed it most.

In 1889, the lodge constructed a two-story brick building on the south side of Main Street. The building was sold in 1973 when the lodge merged with the Kankakee Masonic Lodge.

The Peter Kersch house and barn near Cabery are pictured after the tornado of November 11, 1911. It killed Kersch's 16-year-old son Frank. A tornado in 1903 hit the Patrick Breen farm near Cabery, killing 17-year-old Frank Breen.

The Illinois Central Railroad station in Cabery was a busy place.

The Modern Woodmen of America lodge's drill team in 1903 included, from left to right, George Drew, Thomas Drew, Jacob Drew Sr., William Drew, Jacob Drew Jr., and John Drew.

St. Joseph's Catholic Church started in a log building in 1875. The thriving village started work on a new church in 1904. It was dedicated in 1909. The bishop of Joliet decided to close the church in 2015. Parishioners formed the St. Joseph Preservation Society to keep the building open as a chapel. They raised money to maintain the building, and a doctor promised to buy it. The bishop refused. Parishioners appealed all the way to the Vatican, but they lost. The bishop ordered the church building to be demolished.

What now is Trinity United Methodist Church started out as Cabery Presbyterian Church. A Presbyterian minister from Chicago started preaching in Keyes Hall in 1885. Land was purchased from Edward Clayton in 1886. The church was completed in 1887; the north part was built in 1901. The church joined the Kempton and Campus Methodist churches in 1961 and later became the United Methodist church.

Elmer Colthurst had a fine barn and string of horses at his Cabery farm in 1912.

Cabery's semipro football team, known as the Cabery All-Stars and later the Cabery Independents, won state championships in 1914 and in 1925. Clayton "Dockie" Miller played and coached the team, pictured here in 1910 and 1911. In 1924, Cabery lost only one game, outscoring opponents 133-36. Cabery was undefeated in 1925, outscoring opponents 90-12. Among the teams Cabery defeated was the Decatur Staleys, who had a player/coach named George S. Halas. That team later moved north and changed its name to the Chicago Bears. A historical display honoring the Cabery team is in the National Football League Hall of Fame in Canton, Ohio.

Cabery's football team played Stateville in 1932. The teams fought to a 0-0 tie behind the Joliet prison walls before 300 guests and 3,000 prisoners. The convicts won 12-6 in a rematch. The prison furniture factory is in the background.

Randall Peterson and William Veysey's butcher shop in Cabery is pictured in 1910.

Cabery had baseball teams for men and for women in the 1890s.

Cabery's Main Street is pictured looking east. In its early years, Cabery had as many as 40 businesses, including the Commercial Hotel and saloon, two livery stables, two wagon shops, three blacksmith shops, two lumberyards, three saloons, two restaurants, a flax mill, a steam mill, four general stores, two hardware stores, a furniture store, a drugstore, a clothing store, a butcher shop, two tile factories, a doctor, a dentist, an optometrist, a funeral home, a bowling alley, stockyards, a race track, a creamery, a printing office, a theater, a cheese factory, and two banks.

This game at Cabery's baseball park in 1907 drew a large crowd.

At left is Cabery's early water tower. Below is Cabery Public School in 1907.

Cabery's business district burned down on May 3, 1885, destroying 24 businesses and 14 homes. A solitary figure stands amid the ashes, arms akimbo, wondering what happened. On January 7, 1940, Hallam's grocery store and tavern burned. Mary Jane Hallam, the mother of the family, died in the fire.

Cabery is pictured here in 1898.

Colton School near Cabery is seen in a rare portrait from 1895.

Cabery's first-grade class poses for a picture in 1903.

Cabery High School students face the camera in 1916.

Inside a Cabery store, the man on the right is Everett Quayle.

Cabery High School was built in 1913. Consolidation in 1946 sent Cabery students to Kempton High School. The first eight grades remained in the Cabery building. In 1958, Cabery and Kempton merged. In 1969, Kempton, Cabery, and Cullom merged to form Tri-Point Unit District. In 1972, the Cabery school building was closed. It was demolished in December 2002.

Cabery held a Corn Carnival every October from 1909 to about 1914. The Masonic hall is on the right above. These next few pages show the event through the years.

47

Professional photographers were on hand to record activity at the Cabery Corn Carnival.

Various entertainment delighted crowds at the Cabery Corn Carnival.

The Cabery Corn Carnival was an annual event from 1909 to 1914.

The Cabery Corn Carnival drew large crowds during its short run.

The Corn Carnival on Cabery's Main Street spanned two counties, since Main Street was the dividing line between Ford and Kankakee Counties.

Four

CLARKE CITY AND COAL MINING

In 1900, Clarke City was one of the largest towns in Kankakee County. In less than 20 years, it would completely disappear.

For part of western Kankakee County, coal mining was as important as farming was for the rest of the area. Many boom towns sprang up around mining operations and then disappeared when the mines closed.

Clarke City, Tracy, and Oklahoma were mining towns in Essex Township that started when the coal mines opened in the 1880s.

Clarke City was estimated to have 2,000 people at its peak. Its population declined as mining declined. The population was down to 621 in 1900, but that still was a lot bigger than the 384 in Herscher, 385 in Essex, and 239 in Reddick. The 1900 census numbers showed that Clarke City was the sixth-biggest town in Kankakee County—after Kankakee, Momence, Bradley, St. Anne, and Manteno.

Clarke City started in 1881 when coal mines were developed along the new Kankakee & Seneca Railroad line. The town was named for James C. Clarke, president of the Illinois Central Railroad, because he approved building a spur line from Buckingham to Clarke City, which saved the struggling mine.

Oklahoma was another small coal mining town that no longer exists. It had more than a dozen homes but no businesses. It was a mile south of Clarke City and lasted just a few years in the 1880s.

Tracy was north of Clarke City. Two coal mines opened in 1882; by 1883, there were 40 houses, a school, a number of businesses, and several saloons. There were 200 miners working there in 1885. Its mines closed in 1887, and in 1890, a large number of its houses and stores were moved to Clarke City. The town of Tracy was sold to Emil Freier of Bradley for $57.29 in 1901. Freier, a carpenter, bought the deserted town sight unseen.

Coal mining operations were busy at Clarke City. After mining ended in 1910, houses and stores were picked up and moved. All traces of the town have vanished. Figures from the State of Illinois show that in 1886, there were 73,678 tons of coal mined in Kankakee County. That rose to 97,000 tons the following year. The biggest year for coal mining in the county was 1897, when 180,683 tons were mined. Strip mining began in Essex Township in 1927 and ceased in 1974, with 44 million tons of coal removed from the strip mines in those 47 years. The scars on the land caused by mining later became recreational areas. What had been considered a wasteland was turned into a paradise for fishermen, boaters, hunters, campers, and swimmers. A number of recreational businesses and residential subdivisions were built.

Five

ESSEX

Essex was named by Gardner Royce for his home of Essex County, New York. Royce was one of the earliest settlers, arriving in 1849. The town was officially named Essex in 1880. Before that, the settlement was known as Jackson. The village of Essex was incorporated in April 1885.

In the 1880s, most of the businesses were on north Merchant Street, west of the railroad. The business section gradually moved to the east side. The first store in the village was opened in February 1880 by Christian Albert.

Plans were made for a town hall in 1882. People on both the east and west sides of the tracks wanted it on their side. The west-siders offered a lot for $20. The east-siders offered a lot for free. The west-siders finally won by giving the town a lot for free and $30 cash.

A 1906 account lists Essex's earliest businesses: a town hall, an Odd Fellows hall, an opera house that seated 250, two grain elevators, an electric light plant, two hotels, a livery stable, a drugstore, a hardware store, four general stores, a grocery store, a meat market, a lumberyard, a farm implement store, a furniture store, an undertaker, a steam mill, two blacksmith and repair shops, two millinery stores, a bakery, a confectionery and notions store, a barbershop, a photographer, and a printing shop. Dr. J.W. Allison was the first doctor in Essex, with an office in the Reid Hotel. The practice later was taken by his nephew, Dr. Charles Allison.

A fire on October 12, 1916, destroyed most of the business district on the north side of Main Street—a dry goods store, a general store, a hotel, a bank, a home, a meat market, a soft drink parlor, and a grocery store. New buildings soon went up in their place. Another fire in 1930 destroyed a number of buildings on north Merchant Street, including a saloon, a mortuary, and a furniture store.

Farmers pose with a corn sheller in Essex Township in 1910.

This was the home of Dr. John Allison and his nephew Dr. Charles Allison. They had their office on the first floor and a hospital on the second floor. Dr. John Allison also had offices in Clarke City and South Wilmington.

Essex Grade School, pictured in 1915, was taught by Jennie Engels.

Essex Grade School students are seen here in 1928.

Farmers are shelling corn on the E.A. Scroggins farm in Essex Township in 1902.

A Wabash Railroad train wreck on December 16, 1937, demolished the Essex depot and derailed 33 cars. The Wabash was built through Essex in 1879; it went out of business in 1964. The last passenger service through Essex was on May 1, 1971. The railroad ties were removed in 1991. The Kankakee & Seneca Railroad came through in 1881; it went out of business in 1933.

Men pose in the Ferrero Barber Shop in Essex in the 1930s.

Essex Ladies Aid helped on the home front during World War II.

Henry Schultz is seen driving the hearse for Hasemeyer Funeral Chapel and Furniture Store in Essex in 1909.

The George Hoffman house, near Essex, was built in 1896.

Pictured here are the Essex Methodist Church (left), built in 1906, and St. Lawrence O'Toole Catholic Church, built in 1881.

Frank and Dora Emling pose in front of St. Lawrence O'Toole Church in Essex.

A war memorial was dedicated in Essex in 1944. A new granite memorial replaced this one in 1962.

Six

GOODRICH AND PILOT TOWNSHIP

Goodrich was named for J.L. Goodrich, who granted a parcel of land to the Illinois Central Railroad in 1882 with the stipulation that a station and telegraph office be maintained and that every passenger train was to stop. It was hoped that Goodrich would become a flourishing town on the Illinois Central line. That did not happen.

A plat of a proposed village was drawn in 1883 showing 96 lots and 6 streets. Goodrich had the same potential as many other places that started with a post office, a depot, a grain elevator, a few houses, and a few stores. But fortune passed it by. It is a quiet, serene spot, with only Sacred Heart Catholic Church and a handful of beautiful homes surrounded by peaceful fields.

Nathan Lewis was the first settler, building a house in 1853. He planted a line of trees on the east and south sides of what became the church property. His house was expanded and refurbished by Dr. C.W. Knott, a Kankakee physician who made it his summer home.

Dickey's Siding was not a town but was a clearly identified place. It was important in its time, and it disappeared after it was no longer needed. It was in Pilot Township, three miles east of Herscher. It was named for Sylvester B. Dickey (1836–1929), who built a grain elevator there. A siding is a section of side track going from the main rail to a grain elevator, a mine, or another such site for loading.

Carrow was another fledgling railroad town that no longer exists. Carrow is an Anglicized version of the French name Caron. Pierre Paul Caron (1805–1881) came from Canada to Limestone Township in 1848. His son Joseph Caron/Carrow Sr. (1829–1906) moved to a farm in Pilot Township. There had been a settlement on that land before Carrow came. Joseph Crowley built a stone house in 1862 near a house owned by Joseph Caron/Carrow Sr. The area was known as Cagwin before it was called Carrow.

This is the house built by Nathan Lewis in 1853.

Sylvester B. Dickey (left) was a pioneer settler in Pilot Township. Joseph Carrow Sr. (right) opened a stone quarry in a settlement named for him.

This was the post office at Joseph Carrow's house. He was appointed postmaster in 1883, the same year he opened the Carrow Limestone Rock Quarry along the Three-I Railroad line. A depot was built on his land in 1883. Carrow also started a grain business. In 1906, he sold his company to the Lehigh Stone Company of Kankakee. It moved operations to Limestone Township in 1913. The settlement of Carrow, also known as Old Lehigh, today is gone.

This Our Lady of Fatima shrine is at the Sacred Heart Catholic Church in Goodrich.

The congregation of SS Peter and Paul Catholic Church posed for this picture in 1919. The church was an offshoot of St. James Mission, which was built in 1862 at Carrow. SS Peter and Paul was built in 1869. A schoolhouse was built in 1884.

SS Peter and Paul Catholic School students are seen here in the 1890s.

This was the interior of SS Peter and Paul Catholic Church in Pilot Township. St. James planned in 1894 to move nearer a railroad station. The choice was Irwin, which was primarily Irish. The French decided to build their own church in Goodrich. Since the fundraising and the building were done without the permission of church authorities, the new Sacred Heart congregation was without a pastor until Chicago archbishop P.A. Feehan received the deed to the church property. Fr. Joseph Meyer was named the first pastor of Sacred Heart on June 20, 1899. He served the church for 45 years until his death on May 29, 1944. Father Meyer also was pastor of SS Peter and Paul Catholic Church. It was decided in 1920 to move the church to Herscher. A large brick church was built in Herscher in 1921 and was named for St. Margaret Mary. All that remains on the former SS Peter and Paul property is the Catholic cemetery.

Fr. Joseph Meyer is third from the left in 1942 at a celebration of his 50th year in the priesthood. Cardinal Samuel Stritch is to the right.

Sacred Heart rectory and church in Goodrich are pictured after the steeple blew down in 1996.

The Arthur Appel farm in Pilot Township is seen in 1900.

The Mark Chapman farm on Goodrich Road is seen in 2004 with a Herscher school bus going down the road.

The Johann Mau farm, northwest of Goodrich, is pictured here in 1893.

The Dyvig and Pederson home in Pilot Township is pictured here in 1907.

Seven

HERSCHER

The village of Herscher was named for the man who founded the town. But there was a dispute about how the name was spelled. In the early days, it was Hersher. Today it is Herscher. The original German spelling of the man's name was Herrscher. All three spellings have been used.

John Herscher was born in 1842 in Alsace, France. He arrived in this area in 1855. When the Civil War started, he enlisted in Company F, 156th Illinois Volunteer Infantry. After the war, he returned and started farming and raising livestock. He also became a grain dealer. Herscher's health deteriorated after the war. While he was in a hospital in Chicago, he learned that the Bloomington branch of the Illinois Central Railroad was being planned. He had a hand in bringing the railroad through this area in 1878. Herscher gave the railroad the right of way through his property, and built a hotel for railroad workers and travelers.

As was the story with other towns in the area, it was the Illinois Central's decision to build a station here that established Herscher as a town.

An election on April 26, 1882, approved the incorporation of the village. On May 20, 1882, a board of trustees met in John Herscher's grain office and organized the village. John Herscher was appointed village president.

John Herscher built a grain elevator on Main Street in 1878. A couple of other grain elevators were built in the following years. Herscher's business was later known as Herscher Grain and now is Alliance Grain.

John Herscher laid out the village, graded streets, planted thousands of trees, and set up a park. His house on Main Street was built in 1883 with two etched granite fireplaces, three sets of sliding doors, and four porches. He maintained two dining rooms downstairs for his parties, and planned to use the property behind his house to build a park with a fishpond, deer park, and beer garden. But Herscher's health continued to decline, and he died on May 7, 1885. The Duckworth family owned the house from 1914 to 1972, and Jim and Janet Ridings have owned it since 1984.

In 1872, Azariah Buck opened a store in Pilot Center near Pilot Cemetery, along what is now Route 115. When the railroad came through in 1878, he opened the first store in Herscher. The first post office was in 1865 at Pilot Center in Hiram Aldrich's store. John and Azariah Buck bought Aldrich's store and moved the post office to their store on West Kankakee Avenue in Herscher in 1878.

The Illinois Central Railroad station in Herscher is seen around 1900.

Above are Herscher Public School in 1901 and a view from the school window in 1946. The first classes were on the second floor of a building on the northwest corner of Main and Myrtle Streets in 1880. A schoolhouse was built in 1883 on South Main Street (where senior citizen townhouses are today). In 1900, a high school course was added.

Herscher High School students sit outside the school in 1922.

Herscher High School is shown when it was built in 1924. Additions were built in 1936, 1950, 1967, 1989, and 2001. Herscher formed a unit school district in 1949 to include Pilot, Salina, and Limestone Townships, Buckingham, part of Essex Township, and parts of Ford and Iroquois Counties.

The Herscher High School girls' chorus poses for a yearbook picture in 1939.

74

Wolf and Minnie Leiser are pictured here. Wolf Leiserowitz (1866–1932) came to America from Russia at the age of 20. He started as a peddler, traveling to farmhouses with a pack on his back. He eventually located a store in the stone-front building Walter Hipke built for his drugstore on Main Street. The family shortened its name to Leiser in 1917. The business went from a general merchandise store to a furniture store in 1960. Wolf's son Maurice Leiser served as mayor of Herscher for 28 years (1933–1961), longer than anyone else. He died in 1985 at the age of 91. The baseball field at Pilot Park was named Maurice Leiser Field in 1984. Nearby, a street is named for the family.

Kenneth Seebach (1910–1989) came to Herscher High School as a teacher in 1932 and became principal in 1942. He was the instrumental figure in forming the Unit 2 District in 1949, and became the first superintendent. Seebach retired in 1975. He donated $125,000 in 1978 to build a stadium. The community raised an equal amount of money and contributed material and labor. Kenneth Seebach Stadium opened in 1979.

The Lee building was built in 1898 at Kankakee and Maple Streets. The building burned down on January 8, 1931. John Moore and his family lived upstairs, and Chris Gregorson lived in a rear apartment. Smoke awoke Gregorson at 2:45 a.m. He alerted the Moore family and ran to Arthur Alkire's blacksmith shop next door to get a ladder. He put the ladder to a second-floor window and rescued Moore's wife and their two children. Seventeen-year-old Susanna Piggush had been living with the family as a nursemaid for two weeks. She refused to climb down the ladder and tried to make it down the hall with nine-month-old Leslie Moore. They both died. A year later, Moore's wife confessed that Moore had paid a man to burn down the building while he was out of town. Moore was indicted on two counts of murder, arson, and defrauding an insurance company. These were the only murders in Herscher's history. Moore fled to Oklahoma and changed his name. He died there in 1970. He never was brought to justice.

The biggest day of the year in Herscher is Labor Day. The big parade is followed with a day of food, games, and entertainment in the park. It is called the Herscher Homecoming, a chance for people to come back to Herscher for a reunion with family and friends. But the original intent was to welcome home the men who had fought in World War I. The first Herscher Homecoming was on October 2, 1919, at the war memorial built on Main Street. The event was moved to Labor Day in 1937. Pictured at left is a Labor Day parade float for Herscher Schools in 1928. At right is a 1956 float for Leiser's store with Gerald Hamende and Shirley Loica.

Herscher firemen had water fight competitions on Labor Day for several years. This one was in 1994.

The large bird in this 1925 parade represented Red Goose Shoes, sold at Leiser's.

Janet Schnell (standing) and Betty Ruder (right) are on Herscher's Royal Blue Grocery float in 1956. Lana and Alyce Schnell are sitting up front.

Labor Day always started at the war memorial in the intersection of Main and Kankakee Streets in downtown Herscher, just south of the railroad tracks, as seen in these 1940s pictures. The image above looks north; the one below looks south.

Entertainment has been a part of Labor Day since before this stage was built in 1951. There is nothing but cornfields behind this 1954 performance; the bank, houses, parks, and businesses would be built later.

The 1997 Herscher High School Marching Band won the state championship.

The Herscher Presbyterian Church started in 1879 at Pilot Center, near Pilot Cemetery. A church was built in 1880 on a site donated by John Herscher two blocks north of the business district, where Herscher Grade School is now. The church building was deemed to be too far from town, so it was moved to the southwest corner of Oak Street and Kankakee Avenue in 1888. The church disbanded in 1914.

The Norwegian Lutheran Church began in 1867. Rev. Anders Christian Olsen was the pastor for 37 years until his death in 1906. A church was built in 1882 a mile southwest of Herscher. The 73-foot spire could be seen for miles on the prairie. The church was struck by lightning in 1923 and burned. A new church was built on south Elm Street in Herscher in 1925. Membership declined, and the church disbanded in 1965.

Trinity Lutheran Church started in 1909 when members of Zion Lutheran Church of Bonfield wanted a church in town. They also wanted services in English, and Zion had only German-language services. The church pictured here was dedicated in 1910. A modern church building was completed in 1959.

The Methodist Church came to Herscher in 1887 when the church building at Eldridgeville was dismantled and moved to the northeast corner of Main Street and Myrtle Avenue. It served Herscher Methodists until their own church was built in 1900 on the southeast corner of Main Street and Myrtle Avenue (pictured). The Methodists built a new church on Elm Street in 1965.

Seen here are Herscher Christian Church (left) and St. Margaret Mary Catholic Church. Herscher Christian Church began in 1979. It held services in the Herscher Village Hall until its building was completed in 1988. St. Margaret Mary Catholic Church was built in 1921, after SS Peter & Paul Catholic Church, four miles north of Herscher in Pilot Township, decided to move to town and change its name.

This group picture from 1912 was taken at one of many Armstrong family reunions.

The home of Mayor A.T. Anderson was on the corner of Oak and Myrtle Streets. It later became the Orrison Funeral Home and now is owned by the Herscher Area Historical Society.

The Wolf Leiser house is pictured on North Main Street.

The Herscher Cornet Band posed for this photograph in 1900.

The Theodore Fritz home was on North Main Street in Herscher.

The Herscher Concert Band, seen here in 1918, played patriotic concerts.

Herscher postmaster Frank Whittum and his family are in front of their house at Oak and Myrtle Streets in the 1890s. A second story was later added to the house.

This is the house on Main Street built by John Herscher in 1883.

The Kammann/Wesemann house, on Main and Clyde Streets, was built in 1890.

Above is Main Street in downtown Herscher, looking south in 1908. The tip of the steeple of the Methodist church can be seen in the distance. Below, farmers line up their wagons at the grain elevator. John Herscher's house can be seen in the background.

This is the northwest corner of Main Street at Myrtle Avenue in downtown Herscher.

Pictured is the west side of Main Street in downtown Herscher in 1903.

On the northwest corner of Main Street at Myrtle Avenue was the J.E. Wright General Store, then Citizen's State Bank, Lehman Furniture, and the Herscher Hotel.

This is the interior of Citizen's State Bank on Main Street. The bank opened in 1905 and closed in 1933 during the Great Depression. It later became a restaurant.

The Herscher Hotel is on the left, and the building to the right was a newspaper office and later a bakery; it was torn down and replaced with a brick building that now is a hardware store.

Above, J. Fetterly built his store in downtown Herscher in 1900. It soon became Frank Lehman's furniture and undertaking business. It got a new facade in 1977, when it became Kankakee Federal Savings. It later became a hair salon.

John Klein's harness and shoe repair shop is on the left, a meat market is in the middle, and Walt Hipke's drugstore is on the right.

Here is another view of Herscher's one-block downtown. The wood-frame building on the right with the turret was torn down in 1904, and a third section was added to Hipke's stone-front building.

The State Bank of Herscher was built in 1902. A new building was constructed across the street in 1954. Its present location on Tobey Drive was built in 1979. A branch on Route 17 in Limestone was built in 2003.

Main Street in 1903 shows the hotel built by John Herscher on the right. Next to that is the State Bank of Herscher, the wood-frame drugstore of Huntington James, and the two sections of Walt Hipke's stone-front drugstore.

Here is a scene of downtown Herscher in 1903. The State Bank of Herscher faced a crisis during the Great Depression in 1933. Bank officials went to a Kankakee bank, got a lot of cash, and put it in a big washtub on the floor of the bank so people could see it. Fears were calmed, and the bank survived.

Looking north on Main Street in 1905 shows the Herscher Hotel on the west side of the street and the post office on the east side.

On the east side of Main Street was the post office. The stone-front building, erected in 1898, was a meat market. It was later an auto supply store, a bakery, and a florist shop. The building still stands today.

The barbershop of Thor Fritz, later owned by Bailey Johnson, was on the east side of Main Street. The building was torn down and replaced by the Wagner Garage. The Chevrolet dealership later was just to the north of this.

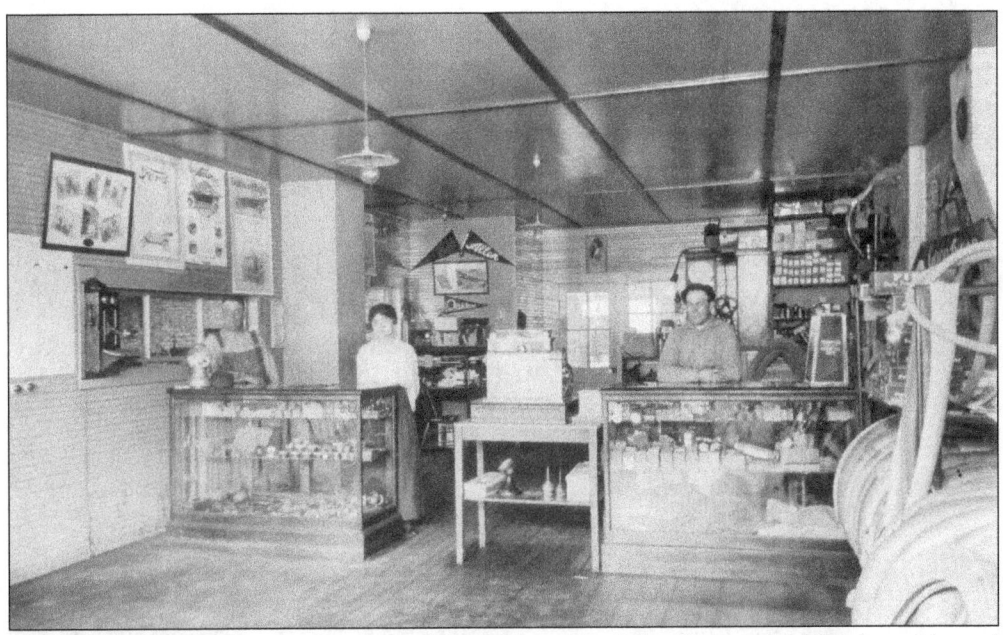

Inside the Wagner Garage in 1916 are, from left to right, John Wagner, Mable Mortveldt, and Adam Wagner.

Heavy snow is seen in this picture looking south on Main Street in the 1920s. The steeple of the Methodist church is in the background on the spot where the present post office stands.

A big snowstorm on Main Street in downtown Herscher was captured in this 1903 photograph.

A photographer captured this scene looking north on Main Street in Herscher.

The east side of Main Street is seen here looking north.

99

The Saffer and Spies Pool Room and the Karcher Hotel and Restaurant were on the southeast corner of Maple Street and Kankakee Avenue in Herscher.

Emile Rabideau's creamery is on the left, on the southeast corner of Main Street and Kankakee Avenue, pictured looking south.

This 1903 picture of Kankakee Avenue, east of Main Street, shows that the business area on that street was as busy as it was on Main Street in that era.

Kankakee Avenue, west of Main Street, shows the Hipke/Leiser building in the background.

Passengers are waiting at the Herscher depot for the train in the distance.

At the north end of Main Street's business district, the creamery building is seen on the corner, and a meat market is north of that.

Two gunmen broke into the State Bank of Herscher early on March 3, 1946. Town police officer Edwin Etzel saw a strange car parked at the bank. He wasn't armed, he said, "Because nothing ever happens in Herscher." As Etzel returned with cashier Walter Payne, the robbers ran out with $10,000 and fired shots at Payne's car. One robber shot a blast from his machine gun, puncturing a tire on Payne's car. Another robber fired a handgun, shattering Payne's windshield. A bullet passed between Etzel and Payne, lodging in the rear of the car. The robbers ordered the two Herscher men into their car, firing another shot in the air to make their point. As they sped north, one of the criminals asked Etzel if he was the local cop. Etzel replied, "I used to be, but not anymore." Etzel resigned as soon as the ordeal ended. The gunmen dropped Etzel and Payne near Oak Lawn. Six men and two women were arrested in Chicago the following day. The police were tipped off by one of the women, who talked out of spite after having a spat with one of the men. In this picture, bank cashier Walter Payne, safe with police protection, points out the armed robbers for newspaper photographers.

Natural Gas Pipeline (now Kinder Morgan) began drilling in 1950 south of Herscher to explore an underground dome created when glaciers carved their way through layers of limestone. The underground dome stores natural gas, piped up from the Gulf Coast for use in the Chicago area. The dome is seven miles long, three miles wide, and covers 8,000 acres. Its capacity is estimated at 90 billion cubic square feet. The first gas was injected into the underground dome beneath Herscher in 1953. Today, it has the capacity to deliver 1.1 billion cubic feet of gas daily. Herscher's first subdivision was a community of 22 homes at the gas plant, built in the early 1950s for the families of plant workers. There were streets, sidewalks, and a community building. A Herscher school bus picked up the schoolchildren who lived there. In the 1960s, these houses were moved into town, and the community building became Herscher's village hall. A section of the natural gas pipeline blew up on March 9, 1956. The flame was so great that it was reportedly seen as far away as Chicago that night. It also created a panic across Kankakee County, as rumors spread that the village of Herscher had blown up. Automatic valves cut off the gas supply, and the fire burned itself out in 45 minutes. The explosion left a crater 60 feet long, 20 feet wide, and 10 feet deep.

Eight

IRWIN AND OTTO TOWNSHIP

By all rights, the town of Irwin should have been called O'Connorville, as was suggested in its early days. There were (and are) so many people there named O'Connor that such a name was only fitting. However, many prospective towns that grew up along a railroad line were better known by the name that the railroad gave to its depot. The depot here was called Irwin Station after George S. Irwin. So that is the name the small town got.

George S. Irwin (1817–1907) married Ruth Stanton in 1845. She was a second cousin of Edwin M. Stanton, secretary of war in Abraham Lincoln's cabinet. The Irwins moved to a farm in Otto Township in 1866 and farmed until 1887, when they moved to Kankakee. A son, Joseph Irwin (1851–1933), was a conductor for the Illinois Central Railroad's line between Bloomington and Kankakee. He started with the railroad in 1876 and helped build that line in 1878, working to secure the right of way and helping with construction.

Michael O'Connor Sr. (1806–1884) and Mary (McMahon) O'Connor (1816–1892) married in Ireland and were the founders of the large O'Connor clan in the Irwin area. The O'Connors bought 160 acres southwest of Irwin in 1868 and farmed with their seven children: Thomas, Michael Jr., Johanna, Mary, William, Timothy, and Maurice. The descendants became so numerous that they were divided into five different clans: the Shanks (Michael Jr.), the Maleys (Thomas and daughter Johanna Maley), the Ferrises (Mary), the Buffaloes (Maurice), and the Bills (William). There are four more nicknamed O'Connor clans—the Bucks, the Prophets, the Mickeys, and the Iowa Jackies—who are not direct descendants of Michael and Mary O'Connor, although they all became related through marriage.

Pictured here are George S. Irwin (left) and Arch Ward. The most famous person from the Irwin area was Arch Ward (1896–1955), born in Irwin to Thomas and Nora Gertrude (O'Connor) Ward. Their home was at Lehigh Road and Route 115. Arch Ward was a sportswriter for the *Chicago Tribune*. He started the all-star baseball game in 1933 and the all-star football game in 1934. He turned down an offer to become head of the NFL. He was inducted into both the Major League Baseball Hall of Fame in Cooperstown, New York, and the National Football League Hall of Fame in Canton, Ohio. The boy from Irwin is the only journalist who has been so honored.

North Irwin School students play outside the school in 1941.

Long-time teacher Doris Devine poses in the cornfields at her Irwin-area home.

Three generations of O'Connor men, all named William, are pictured in 1916: grandfather (1849–1919), son (1884–1954), and grandson (1914–2010).

The St. James rectory and church in Irwin were built in 1895 on an acre of land donated by Michael O'Connor. A tornado on April 2, 1982, destroyed the building. A new church was built in 1983.

Sacred Heart Catholic School in Irwin was built by St. James Catholic Church in 1918. The school closed in 1965 and was demolished in 1978.

Jerry Graney's saloon in Irwin is pictured here in 1910.

Irwin's east grain elevator is seen it its early days.

The Michael O'Connor clan posed for this picture in front of their Irwin homestead.

Alex O'Connor farms with horses at the age of 15 in 1933.

The Irwin Bank is seen in the early 1900s in this picture.

The Irwin Hall and the Irwin Bank are pictured here. Burglars broke into the Irwin Bank on the night of November 25, 1919. They got in through an unlocked window and used nitroglycerin to blow open the vault. They stole $8,000 in Liberty Bonds. There was a second bank in town, Irwin State Bank, in the 1920s.

The Irwin Cash Store was a popular local business.

Nine

LEHIGH

Lehigh is one area in Kankakee County that has been located in two different spots. The area known as Carrow and later as Old Lehigh was in Pilot Township. Lehigh Stone Company operated a quarry there and later moved operations a little farther south into Limestone Township.

Lehigh is also the one area in the county named for an industry rather than a man or a railroad stop. There was never a village of Lehigh. There is just the Lehigh Stone Company on Lehigh Road and an area once known as Old Lehigh. There was a Catholic church and a cemetery there, both of which are now gone.

The Lehigh quarry started a few miles northwest of its present site in Pilot Township, east of Goodrich. The Three-I Railroad was built across the northern part of Pilot Township in 1881 and 1882, and a station was set up along the line. This was called Carrow after the owner of the land, Joseph Carrow. He began a limestone quarry on his land in 1883.

Michael Edgeworth and W.R. Sanborn bought what they called "a useless little 13 acres of land" at the railroad station at Carrow. Lehigh Stone Company was incorporated on June 1, 1906. However, in 1916, it appeared the quality of the stone was limited. Sanborn found an area of unbroken stone about a mile southeast, in Limestone Township. Quarrying began in 1917. Tracks were laid to connect to the Illinois Central Railroad near Irwin.

The Lehigh quarry produces the highest-quality dolomite limestone found anywhere. Stone from Lehigh has been used in building countless miles of roads and many buildings in the area and at Rantoul Air Force Base, Memorial Stadium at the University of Illinois, and more.

Lehigh today is not much more than the stone quarry and adjoining farmland. But it used to be a community of several homes, a tavern, and a store. There was a Lehigh community for many people who worked at the quarry.

The Pilot Township quarry was the scene of a Mafia hit in April 1925. Sam Vaccero, a Kankakee bootlegger and gangster, was found shot to death inside a car in 30 feet of water. Two days after Vaccero's body was found, two other gangsters were murdered in Kankakee in retaliation.

Visitors observe the stone crusher at the Lehigh quarry.

The Lehigh quarry was photographed by Powell Studio of Kankakee in 1908.

115

Pictured is part of the Lehigh community in the 1950s. Five railroad workers at Lehigh were killed on August 3, 1929, while working on the railroad bed just east of Lehigh Road. The noise from the air compressor was so loud that they did not hear an approaching train. The train hit the work crew, tearing them to bits and scattering them about. In April 1996, actor Keanu Reeves shot scenes for his movie *Chain Reaction* at the quarry. A Hollywood crew of 250 people filmed there for three days. The monumental scope of the quarry was the reason it was chosen for the scenes. Rescue crews from the Limestone Fire Department and other departments were called to save two women who were trapped while trying to scale the quarry's cliffs on February 1, 2021. The women were caught 80 feet above the ground on a snowy and icy spot on unstable stone. Kankakee Fire Department lieutenant Dave Wiechen rappelled 100 feet from the top to put a harness on the women so they could be pulled out with ropes.

Ten

Limestone

Limestone Township got its name from the limestone rock stratum that dominates the area and that has provided the material, from quarries in the township, for everything from building foundations to roads.

The Hawkins brothers—Robert, Joel, Micah, and Alanson—moved into the Limestone area in 1834 and built the first house there that year. This is the first mention of a settlement in western Kankakee County.

A surveyor who had seen the area was in Danville, and he told the Hawkins men about it. Alanson and Micah rode here by oxcart in 1832 to take a look and made camp near the spring on Squaw Creek. They liked what they saw. Micah stayed, while Alanson went to Chicago to stake a claim. The Limestone area was known as Hawkins Grove and then was a part of Iroquois County. Micah Jepson Hawkins is considered the second white settler in Kankakee County, after Noel LeVasseur in Bourbonnais, who came here a few months earlier in 1832.

The first school was taught in the home of Alanson Hawkins in 1835 by his sister Sabra (who later married George Byrnes). The first schoolhouse in the Limestone area was built of logs in 1841.

The Byrnes family produced three sheriffs. George Byrnes was the first sheriff of Kankakee County, and his brother James was the second. Arthur, the son of James, was sheriff in the 1890s.

A few early settlers include Hawkins, Nichols, Shreffler, Byrnes, Bracken, Bratton, Butz, Powell, Dahm, Heil, Wiley, Falter, Tanner, and Yeates.

Quarrying of limestone started in 1853, when the Illinois Central Railroad opened a quarry at Wiley's Creek. The railroad built a depot in 1853 in what would become Kankakee. The railroad brought laborers to Limestone to vote illegally to establish Kankakee County; another election rigged by the Illinois Central made Kankakee the county seat.

Limestone was the first township in Kankakee County. However, the oldest township became the newest village when it incorporated in 2006, largely to avoid having portions annexed to the City of Kankakee.

Micah Jepson Hawkins (left) was one of the first settlers in Limestone. George Byrnes (right) was the first sheriff of Kankakee County.

Micah and Harriet Hawkins pose in front of their second house, built in the 1840s.

This 1883 rendering shows the Shreffler farm, owned by one of the dominant families of Limestone Township.

From left to right, Irene, Wade, and Iona Hawkins were the children of Micah Jepson Hawkins Jr.

Limestone Grade School was heavily damaged by a fire on December 1, 1966. Firemen fought the blaze for four hours in zero-degree weather. Three firemen were injured. The loss was estimated at $220,000.

A fire at Phillips Pipeline on December 14, 1969, sent a fireball 35 feet high. The well held 10 million gallons of propane. There were 150 firefighters with 16 trucks on the scene for 87 hours. Firefighters pumped 2.6 million gallons of water.

The barn on the Falter farm in Limestone Township was built in 1867.

The Louis Dahn farm in Limestone Township is pictured here.

Micah and Harriet Hawkins sit in their buggy on the bluff overlooking the Kankakee River in the 1890s.

David Hawkins and family pose in 1911 on the Hawkins homestead.

The Luther Bratton home in Limestone Township was built in 1866.

This barn on Warner Bridge Road was built in 1877 by Thomas Smith. It is 36 by 46 feet with a basement wall 8 feet high. It was later owned by the Riegel and Rieke families.

This was the first farmhouse of John and Pearl Butz in Limestone Township.

Warner Bridge Road (pictured just after the bridge was built in 1920) is the dividing line between Limestone and Salina Townships. The bridge crosses the Kankakee River at the state park. Originally, the area was known as Hanford's Landing. Farmers hauled their grain a great distance to Wilmington or Kankakee until Stephen Hanford built a grain elevator on the south side of the river in 1874. Warner's Landing was on the north side.

Limestone Township graduates in 1917 sit with their teacher, Sue Dubois.

Students at Bracken School in Limestone Township were taught by Amy Tanner in 1933.

The old Hawkins School, seen here in 1912, was built in the late 1870s. It was torn down and replaced with a brick school in 1933 on what is now Route 17. It still stands and is today a residence.

Balthazor School in Limestone Township, seen here in 1932, was among the one-room schoolhouses that were known by the name of the farmer who donated the land for the school.

Birdie Davis (far left) played several instruments and entertained local audiences for decades. She married Henry Davis (in front) in 1907.

Dreamland was a popular entertainment spot on Route 17 just west of Limestone School Road. It was in a large building and had a neon sign.

Students of the Mapes one-room school in Limestone Township are seen in this 1911 photograph. Mapes School was built of local limestone in 1842 near Wiley Creek and the Kankakee River, along what would become Route 113.

Students at the Rathman School in Limestone Township line up for this 1920s photograph.

Women are shown preparing for an event at the Limestone Jolly Club in 1909. It was one of several social clubs in Limestone Township.

The South Limestone Social Circle posed for this 1929 portrait. The club started in 1922.

The As You Like It Club gathers for its 40th anniversary in 1948.

From left to right, George Rathman, Fred Goodknecht, and Will Naese share their wisdom about farming in Limestone Township in July 1948.

Eleven

REDDICK

There is no definite proof of how the village of Reddick got its name. But there certainly is a colorful legend, even if it is untrue.

Before it became a town, the locale was known informally as Shellyville, Fellerville, and Ben Moe after some of the first settlers. A post office opened in May 1880 with the name Ben Moe. It changed its name to Reddick in September 1880.

The first of two railroad lines was built in 1879 near the spot where the village now stands. This was the Wabash Railroad, which went from Chicago to St. Louis. Henry Shelly gave the Wabash Railroad the land for a right of way and a depot.

The second railroad, built in 1882, was the Indiana-Illinois-Iowa Railroad, known as the Three-I Railroad. It went from Momence to Streator. This line later became part of the New York Central and then the Penn Central.

The town was platted in 1880 by Henry Shelly, who is considered the founder of the town.

For years, a local legend that was taught in the grade school said that the village was named for a friendly railroad man named Dick, who went by the nickname "Red" because of his red hair. Red Dick reportedly worked on building the Three-I Railroad. Naming the town for this man, according to the legend, was a compromise among many citizens who thought the town should be named for them.

However, the town got the name of Reddick in 1880, two years before Red supposedly came to the area to work on the Three-I Railroad.

Why Reddick? There was a prominent man at that time named William Reddick. But no one knows if he had any connection to this village. William Reddick lived in Ottawa. Until 1870, this area was in the same congressional district as Ottawa. Also, William Reddick was on the board of trustees of the Eastern Hospital for the Insane in Kankakee. It is possible he passed through this area on his way from Ottawa to Kankakee several times from 1877 until his death in 1885.

A train derailment and explosion in Reddick killed three people on June 4, 1907. As the train left the tracks, a carload of dynamite exploded, sending pieces of iron and wood flying for a mile. A large section of the track was blown up, and a hole 16 feet deep and 60 feet in diameter was blown into the ground. Glass windows in businesses and homes in Reddick were blown out.

Significant fires hit Reddick in 1882, 1895, 1904, and 1916, destroying most of the business district each time. A fire that started in the back of the M.F. Reilly General Store (pictured) in 1895 destroyed an entire block of 19 businesses. The fire on October 26, 1904, was the 17th fire in the town's history.

The Wabash stationmaster had a unique way of getting down the tracks.

Above, guests celebrate the wedding of Adam and Elsie Oesterle in 1906. At left is the Reddick Grade School. It was built in 1902 and demolished in 1988.

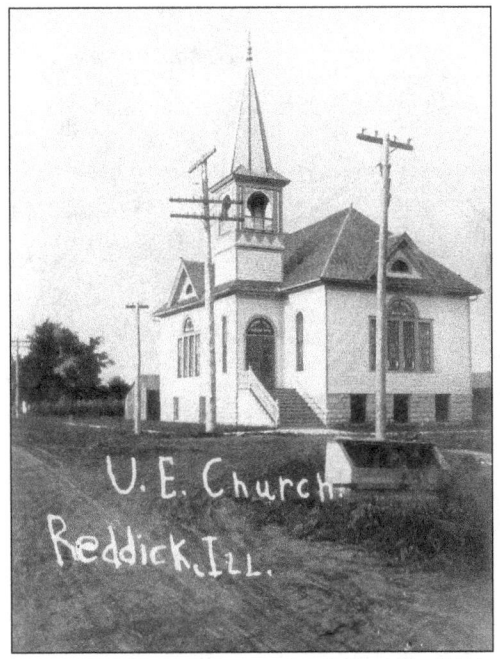

Immanuel United Evangelical Church (left) was built in 1893. It united with the Methodist church in 1968. At right is the Methodist Episcopal church's first building. A new church is on the Reddick curve.

At left is Zoar's first building. It built a new church on Route 17 in 1973. St. Mary's Catholic Church (right) still stands today.

There was a lot of damage from the tornado of 1912.

William Unz's general store also sold Wheeler and Wilson sewing machines.

Reddick School in 1902 was taught by Nellie Shimmin and Laura Hasemeyer.

The Shimmin School was near Reddick in 1904.

The first school in the village of Reddick was built in 1902. A two-year high school started in 1906. A high school district was established in 1915, and classes were held from 1915 to 1921 in the Century Building. The high school building (pictured) was constructed in 1921. Declining enrollment and a declining tax base ended the district in 1988. It was annexed into the Herscher School District. The Reddick High School building was razed in 1998.

Reddick High School had a fleet of school buses in 1935.

Reddick High School students pose in 1920. The girl standing directly behind the boy second from the left is Irma Unz.

Reddick High School's basketball team is seen here in 1927.

This was the Reddick High School senior class in 1925.

This was Reddick High School's third-floor study hall in 1924. Reddick Junior College was established in 1933 from a grant to provide further education to those who could not find work during the Depression. The grant money ran out after two years. There was not another junior college in the county until Kankakee Community College started in 1966.

Reddick High School's 1947 football team went 8-0 and was one of the few undefeated teams in the state. It might have won the state championship if a playoff system had been in effect. The Bulldogs had the highest scoring rank per game of any football team in the state of Illinois.

The Unz family farmed northeast of Reddick, seen in this 1931 photograph.

At left, Irma Unz (1904–2000) was a teacher and principal for 53 years. She started as a grade school student in 1909 and lived to see the school demolished, as seen below in 1998.

This is what was left of the Nelson Hulse house after the tornado of 1912, which killed Hulse, his wife, and his two young daughters.

Russ Schultz peeks from the window of his gas station on the Reddick curve in 1940.

The Reinhart Shelly farm is pictured in 1894.

An early Fourth of July parade heads up Shelly Avenue.

The Reddick Cornet Band stands in front of the Reddick State Bank in the early 1900s. The bank opened in 1903 and closed in 1933 during the Great Depression. The building later became a tavern.

Lincoln Street in Reddick is seen here.

Wabash Avenue is pictured in 1912. The middle building is Michael Reilly's store, and the building on the right is the Reddick State Bank. In 1903, Reddick had four churches, a tile factory, two grain elevators, a millinery and dressmaker shop, a general store, a livery stable, two hotels, a lumber and coal business, a barbershop, a blacksmith shop, a funeral home, and other businesses.

The men outside the Pedersen and Schultz saloon and buffet jokingly hold a handbill favoring Prohibition.

The west side of Wabash Avenue is shown with the Pedersen and Schultz saloon on the left. The middle store has a sign that reads "Geo. Hulbert Pianos." On the right is the B.F. Hertz furniture store and undertaking business.

Looking east, the Methodist church steeple can be seen on the left.

The photographer's postcard reads "Looking west on Main Street," but it is looking east, with Reddick Grade School in the distance.

Twelve

Union Hill and Norton Township

The town of Union Hill was named in a patriotic gesture to a nation that was being torn apart by the Civil War. John E. Schobey, the founder of the town, wanted the word "union" in the name of his settlement's post office to signify the union of North and South.

Several names were suggested. Union Grove was proposed to postal authorities in Washington, DC. But because there already was a town in Illinois with that name, it was decided the name would be Union Hill, since there was a very slight elevation on the flat farmland.

The first man to homestead the land was Cornelius Schobey, John's brother. John Schobey opened a store in 1861. John Robinson erected a gristmill in 1882, a general store was built by G.P. Smith, and a grain elevator was built by A.G. Smith in 1884. Grand Prairie Grain Cooperative was formed in 1888. The Union Hill Farmers Elevator Company started in 1922.

The railroad played a vital role in establishing Union Hill. In 1882, the Indiana-Illinois-Iowa Railroad was built through John Schobey's property in Norton Township, and a town started to be built.

There were two banks in town, the Bank of Union Hill and Farmers Bank of Union Hill.

A meeting place was built in 1895. It was known as Woodmen Hall, but the lodge only rented it. A Modern Woodmen of America lodge was active for many years, and annual Halloween oyster suppers and card parties were held in the hall. The lodge disbanded in 1937, and the Union Hill Hall Association was formed with new members. The Lions Club took title to the building in 1969.

There was no church building in Union Hill, but services and Sunday school were held in the community hall for more than 50 years. In the late 1890s, church services and Sunday school were held in the Woodmen lodge building.

John Schobey (left) was the founder of Union Hill. At right, people wait outside the Union Hill depot in this 1910 photograph.

The Bartlett Frazier grain elevator, the depot, and the Van Voorst coal sheds are seen here.

Damage in Union Hill was great from the tornado of November 11, 1911.

A threshing ring on the Andrew Ruder farm in Norton Township takes a break. The township was named for Jesse O. Norton of Joliet, an attorney who was the congressman from that area from 1853 to 1857. Norton and Pilot Townships had been called the Grand Prairie because it was almost all flat land.

E.J. Baker, the railroad station agent, stands in front of George Van Voorst's lumber sheds next to the railroad tracks.

Ed Sutter opened his store in Union Hill in 1917. Sutter's was a grocery store, ice cream parlor, gas station, farm produce store, and department store for 65 years. It is pictured here in 1934. Ed Sutter operated his store until he died in 1981.

The Adam Seagar house is pictured here on South Street in Union Hill.

153

Union Hill School is pictured here in 1927. Norton Township one-room schoolhouses were Dublin, Reddick, Patchett, Reed, Ellsworth, Duffy, Beardsley, Nutt, Grimwood, Clifford, Union Hill, and Colton.

Union Hill School (pictured in 1963) closed in 1966. Students then went to Reddick. Union Hill became part of Herscher's school district in 1988. The former Union Hill School building burned down in 1981.

Grades one to four in Union Hill's two-room schoolhouse are pictured in 1918. The Union Hill School at first featured eight grades and two years of high school.

This was Union Hill School in the 1940s.

Union Hill's train station was a busy spot.

Union Hill's baseball team is pictured in 1917. As early as 1875, baseball was played here when a team from Union Hill hosted the Modocs of Pogsonville.

George Van Voorst is seen on the right supervising a bridge-building crew in Norton Township about 1900. Van Voorst came to Union Hill in 1886 as a station agent and telegrapher for the Three-I Railroad. He later became a grain dealer and bridge builder and established the family lumber business. In more than 100 years of its history, Union Hill has had just four mayors: George Van Voorst, 1904 to 1936; his son Gilbert, 1936 to 1978; Gilbert's son Hugh, 1978 to 2018; and Hugh's son Grant since 2018.

Arsene Beauclerc's blacksmith shop in Union Hill is on the left. The shop to the right was the wagon and buggy paint shop.

August G. Smith opened this store in 1888. It was later operated by the Desens brothers and eventually became the main office of Van Voorst Lumber. It burned in the big fire of 2019.

Here is a view inside A.G. Smith's store, which was later the Van Voorst office.

Union Hill's big fire was on August 9, 2019. VanFab, the manufacturing arm of Van Voorst Lumber, burned to the ground. The 7,000-square-foot complex of buildings was more than a block long. Fire departments from 35 communities responded, using more than 200,000 gallons of water taken from a nearby pond. Flames shot 100 feet in the air. Damages exceeded $10 million, and insurance covered most of the loss. Within a few days, a trailer was brought in for offices. Space for manufacturing was rented in other locations, and some work was subcontracted. All the data was backed up, so the company was back up and running quickly. The first order shipped three weeks after the fire.

Visit us at
arcadiapublishing.com

CPSIA information can be obtained
at www.ICGtesting.com
Printed in the USA
BVHW091732231221
624747BV00003B/181